Gods and Consciousness

mapping the development of consciousness
through views of ultimacy

by Doug Kraft

Table of Contents

Forward

It has been enriching and fun to have known Doug Kraft since 2000, when I was serving a church in Silicon Valley and he was called as Lead Minister by the Unitarian Universalist Society of Sacramento. We have served together as officers for the UU ministers' association in the Pacific Central District. Our colleagues look to him as a pastor to pastors, coach, accompanist, troubadour, trouble-shooter, neck massager, sophisticated psychotherapist, and wise elder. He's a compassionate and mellow court jester.

Little did I know when I left this District in 2007 that I would return in a year to serve along with Doug, in an associate ministry position at this church.

He's gone beyond merely recruiting me to the job. He helped me set up an old futon frame and a new laptop computer, drill holes in my wall and move old furniture in and out of a two-story apartment. As a colleague and leader, he's loyal, collaborative and playful. He's open to being challenged and is thoughtful in challenging me. He's insightful about human nature and forgiving of human blind spots and slip-ups, including mine.

In few parish pastors have I seen such a balance of ministerial talents as we have in Doug. He stays on top of the facts and figures of the institution's life and history, and he counsels individuals with care and insight. He supports the nuts and bolts of board and committee work while keeping our long-range vision, goals and congregational covenant in front of our eyes. He leads us in song with his guitar, delivers dharma talks, and keeps his church data organized and handy on multiple software applications he created himself. He *devotes heavy amounts of time to reading, sermon preparation and rehearsal, and his daily meditation practice.*

Doug doesn't talk much in his sermons about our Unitarian Universalist spiritual forbears or progressive theological heritage, even though he grew up as a UU in Houston and has served in historic churches in New England and in Sacramento, where Unitarianism arrived not long after the Gold Rush. Instead, Doug embodies our tradition. The Unitarian minister professor of social ethics James Luther Adams (among others) has said that one of the keys to liberal religion is that revelation is not sealed, but continuous. New insights and understandings about God and human life continue to develop.

So it is that Doug has introduced our congregation to his ideas and those of Ken Wilber about human consciousness and spiritual literacy. These four sermons invite us to consider how human beings perceive the divine and one another, and how we think about thinking about God.

The sermons are not only rich in analysis and thought, they use vivid examples and stories. They are compassionate, practical and helpful—as he strives to make all his sermons, and all of his ministry. Doug invites us to let go of the prize of certainty and the illusion of control. He invites us to ease up a bit, step back, observe, and relax. What an invitation. What a sweet and simple gift.

Roger D. Jones, Family Minister
Sacramento, June 2011

Gratitude

I'm grateful to Bruce Moulton of my congregation in Sacramento for encouraging me and helping underwrite the production of this book.

Helping to edit the text were Linda Klein, Eileen Karpeles and Cassandra Opiela.

I'm also grateful to my congregation whose generous and probing listening helped me shape these thoughts. As always I'm eternally thankful to my wife, Erika, who read and critiqued all this material in its formative stages.

Doug Kraft
Sacramento, June 2011

Introduction

Ray leaned over his desk working fervently on his sermon. He'd been serving the congregation since graduating from a Unitarian Universalist seminary a little over a year before. He thought of himself as "spiritual without being religious." His progressive religion didn't provide answers – it encouraged people to find their own. Ray was grateful for this as he poured himself into shaping his message.

Meanwhile, Jimmy, Ray's six-year-old son, wandered into the little study. He saw his dad working away and knew enough not to disturb him. Instead, he walked to the window and gazed out.

It was raining that morning. The wind blew the trees as raindrops splattered the window and

rivulets meandered beside the road. The sky was puffy grey.

After a few minutes he asked aloud, "Daddy, why is there anything?"

Ray looked up from his desk without turning around. His sermon crumbled to dust. His mind went blank. This wasn't a flash of insight. It was a cloud of unknowing. He hadn't a clue as to how to answer his son's simple question.

He turned to Jimmy who was still gazing at the blustery world. "I don't know," Ray said.

Something in Ray's tone caught Jimmy's attention. He turned and looked at his dad. "It's okay," he said. "I just wondered." He walked over, gave his dad a hug and walked out of the room.

Ray didn't get any more writing done that morning.

The traditional answer to Jimmy's question is, "God did it." For some, this answer is satisfying and comforting. For others it's neither. It just kicks the metaphysical can down the road without answering anything. It raises more questions: "Why did God do it?" "Why is there God?" "If God was here before anything else, where did God come from?" "What made God?" "And what made whatever made God?" "Why is there anything?"

Those who don't embrace this kind of God may turn to science for explanations: complex creatures evolved from simpler creatures and simpler creatures evolved from the earliest life and organic matter evolved from inorganic matter and it all started with a Big Bang a long, long time ago. However, this doesn't answer the question either. It explains how things evolved but doesn't answer why there is anything to evolve in the first place.

Sooner or later we confront simple, basic questions about existence for which we have no answers. They may come from a theological professor, a beloved progeny, the stillness of a star-filled night or the contemplation of a stormy morning. We may ponder these deeply or brush them aside. But they arise.

Perhaps God language first arose in the attempt to speak about such things – to speak about that which is beyond our capacities to articulate clearly.

I am a Unitarian Universalist minister and long-time student of Buddhist meditation among other things. I rarely talk to my congregation using God language other than to share stories like the one about Ray and Jimmy. I find the language confusing. For some, the word "God" touches what is most deeply real and meaningful. For others it touches painful memories of being judged or made to feel guilt. For others it sounds like intellectual childishness.

So I usually steer clear of God language and look for ways to share direct experiences.

However, if we are to engage in conversations with people across the religious spectrum (much less across the political spectrum), it's helpful to have language that is both embracing and discerning. To develop this, we must look at the consciousness that is engaging the issues.

In the Spring of 2011 I decided to see what I could contribute to that engagement. The results are in the following pages which were originally delivered as sermons. They are collected here under the title "Gods and Consciousness" not because there are pantheons of gods out there in the universe but because there are pantheons of gods "in here" in the collective human consciousness. Understanding these various "gods" gives us clues to understanding the structures of our own and other's consciousness and the ways we assign meaning to our experience.

Each talk contained a short recap of the previous material. I've left these in the book form in hopes they will underline key ideas and experiences as I expand on them.

1. Circle of Caring

Compassion and empathy are much needed in our personal lives and in the world. A central question of compassion is "Who is included in our circle of caring?"

• Does it include just our own so-called better qualities (like caring and thoughtfulness) and exclude our worse qualities (like anger and impatience) as not worthy of compassion? Or does it include everything in our beings?

• Does it extend beyond to include loved ones in the way a parent may care more for their child's well-being than for their own?

• Does it expand to include those in a group we identify with – our religious community, political party, ethnic group, home country – and exclude everyone outside this group as less important?

• Does it include people today but not future generations – our children's children?

• Does it include all humans but not other life forms?

These are not abstract questions. Today the recession has created many difficulties. We hear politicians and people on the street intone, "In these hard times we have to deal with reality first. We have to deal with what's important first. The rest are luxuries we can't afford now."

They say this as if it's obvious what's most fundamental and everyone ought to agree with them. But the query "What is ultimately most real?"

and "What is ultimately most important?" are deep theological, philosophical and spiritual queries.

Different views of God or ultimate reality give very different answers as to what is most important in life and who or what is in our circle of caring and who or what is to be jettisoned as unessential.

God

So this morning we're going to talk about God. This is the first in a series on a topic Unitarian Universalist find a little dicey. We have no trouble with politics, sex or money. But God makes us a little squeamish.

So let's get right to it: what is God? Let's start with you. When you hear the word "God," what thoughts, images and associations come to mind?

Old bearded gentleman
Charles Heston before an enflamed shrub
Impersonal force of love in the universe
Everything that is
Jesus dying on the cross
Something I pray to
Giver of life
...

The first thing we can say about God is that He/She/It has many different costumes. So when somebody says "I believe in God" or "I don't believe in God," she isn't telling us anything interesting. A more interesting question is "What form of God do you believe in or don't believe in?"

An atheist is someone who doesn't believe in a *particular* form of God. The early Christians were called atheists for rejecting the old Roman gods.

Centuries later, pagans were called atheists for not embracing a Christian form of God.

In other words, all of us are atheists: there are some – probably many – views of God that we don't adhere to.

And all of us believe in some form of God. When asked, "What is ultimately most real?" or "What is ultimately most important in life?" all of us can come up with some answer. We may have to sort out the language and find vocabulary we find acceptable: "God," "Spirit," "nature," "highest truth," "the Universe." But all of us have some sense of ultimacy. That is our functional equivalent of God by whatever name.

1st, 2nd and 3rd Person

To begin sorting out these costumes of God (or anything else for that matter), let's consider three perspectives from which we might view God or anything.

One is to look inside ourselves – an internal perspective. Second is to consider how we relate to what's out there – a relational perspective. Third is to look outside ourselves – an external or objective perspective.

Ken Wilber,[1] the philosopher who inspired much of this material, refers to these views as 1st person, 2nd person and 3rd person.

---

[1] Ken Wilber is a prolific writer. A good introduction to his work as it relates to this material is *Integral Spirituality* (Integral Books: Boston and London, 2007) and an audio recording called *One Two Three of God* (*Sounds True*, www.soundstrue.com).

As you may recall from grammar school, first person is the one speaking, second person is the one spoken to and third person is the one spoken about. "I," "we" and "us" are first person. "You," "y'all" and "you guys" are second person. And "he," "she," "it" and "them" are the third person.

All cultures and languages have these perspectives built in. They refer to realms of experience we all know. We study them in different ways.

For example, art is the realm of the first person. What's most important in art is how something touches us. The same painting or music may strike each of us differently. "Art is in the eye (or 'I') of the beholder."

Morals and ethics are the second person realm. They focus on how I treat you and how you treat me.

Science is the third person realm. A scientist becomes a disinterested third person observing phenomena as impersonal "its."

What's most important: an internal view, a relational view or an objective view? ...

It's a trick question. It's like asking, "Which is better: art, morals or science?"

All are important. They're just different perspectives. Any complete view of reality or God must take all three into account, preferably without confusing them. We live in all three all the time. We all have feelings and perceptions. We all relate to one another. And we all observe the world around us.

Internal, relational and objective. First, second and third person. Art, ethics and science.

Sorting God

Now let's go back to the question of what is most real or most important. I asked what the word "God" meant to you. We can sort answers into the three perspectives.

Some of your responses were internal or first person: "still small voice within," my deepest experience, a feeling that arises inside, my true nature, Buddha nature, Christ nature, soul, and so forth.

Some of you answered relationally or in the second person: the one I address in prayer, the one I speak to when I'm confused. Compassion and love refer to ways we relate.

And some of you answered in the objective third person: forces that move through the universe, nature, the manifest world.

Sorting Traditional Paths

All the major spiritual traditions answer the question of God or Spirit in the first, second and third person.

Hinduism, for example, has Jana yoga which contemplates the nature of self – first person/internal. It has Bhakti yoga – second person devotional relationship to the divine. And it has Karma yoga working with impersonal laws of how things work – third person.

Buddhism has the three jewels or refuges: Buddha, Dharma and Sangha. Buddha refers to our Buddha nature – first person. Dharma refers to the laws of how the universe operates – third person. And Sangha refers to the community of seekers – second person relationships.

Classical Christianity has a Trinity: Father, Son and Holy Spirit. God the Father is someone we relate to in prayer – second person. God the Son is our inner Christ nature – first person. And the Holy Spirit is an impersonal divine force that permeates the universe – third person.

Unitarian Universalism has seven principles. The first is the inherent worth and dignity of every person – first person. The seventh principle is the interdependent web of life – third person. Between these are five other principles which include justice, equity, compassion, democratic process, peace and liberty – how we relate to one another in the second person.

In this congregation, some of us are looking for happiness or well-being – first person internal. Some are looking for community and ways to relate more deeply – second person relational. Some want to bring more justice and equity into the world – third person systems. Some of us are looking for a mixture of all three of these.

Unfolding

One way to begin to sort out the costumes of God is to ask, "From which perspective is God, Spirit or ultimate reality viewed – 1st person/internal, 2nd person/relational or 3rd person/objective?"

As we deeply engage in any one of these perspectives, it unfolds. We evolve in a natural developmental progression.

Another way we can sort out God, Spirit or ultimacy is developmentally. Some views are young – appropriate for a child, beginner or novice. Other views are more nuanced and complete. They're appropriate for an adult or sage.

This maturation begins with a sense of separation between us and the ultimate. We may be in communion with God or nature, but they are wholly other. Even if we talk with them, there is significant distance between us and God or Goddess.

In the middle range of development, God, Spirit or ultimate reality is more intimate. We are less like spectators and more like lovers in union.

In the higher ranges, we merge with God, Spirit or the universe. We are at One with them. Our self-identification no longer stands apart.

This developmental trajectory goes from separateness to connection to oneness. Ken Wilber calls it communion to union to identification. The Jewish mystic Martin Buber might call it "I-it" to "I-Thou" to "I-I."[2]

---

[2] Martin Buber, *I Thou*, (Charles Scribhner's Sons, New York, 1958). Martin Buber talks about I-it and I-Thou relationships. The I-I is my own extrapolation of his language to and even deeper merging.

Matrix Map

The map on the next page gives three perspectives – internal, relational and objective or 1st, 2nd and 3rd person. It also gives us three levels of maturity – separateness, connection and oneness. If we put them together we have a three by three matrix with nine addresses or nine costumes. All nine are legitimate though some are more evolved. All nine are distinct and yet relate to each other in the matrix map.

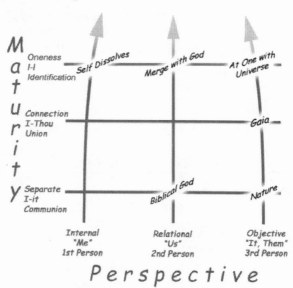

Third Person

To make this more personal, let's look at how consciousness unfolds along one perspective. We'll start with the third person because it is quite common among Unitarian Universalists. In the next talk we'll look at the second and first person.

In the modern world as traditional images of God faded, nature emerged as ultimate reality. Today, science may give us the most familiar third person view of life. Many people believe the physical universe is the fullest manifestation of reality. Instead of calling it "God," ultimate reality is called "nature."

3rd Person Separate

Classical Newtonian physics sees the universe as a massive collection of impersonal objects interacting through impersonal laws. Like billiard balls bouncing off one another, we may contact each other and communicate. But we remain essentially separate.

This is a third person separate view of ultimate reality.

Martin Buber gives an example of looking at a tree and noticing its shape, color and beauty. The tree remains just a tree – a separate object. He calls this an I-it relationship.

Deism is another third person separate view. Deists believe a Deity set the universe in motion and then withdrew. He no longer tinkers with the universe. The Deist God is not one we can pray to because He isn't listening. The divine forces of love or creativity are separate from us. Our job is to understand and live harmoniously within these forces.

3rd Person Connection

If we engage the natural world more deeply, we move from separateness to connection. What might this look like?

Many of you say, "My religion is nature" – a third person perspective. Perhaps you walk in the woods or mountains or watch the stars on a clear night. This helps you enjoy the marvelous web of life.

Then there are moments when you don't feel quite so separate. You aren't just a spectator. There's more going on than can be seen in a photograph. There's a deeper connection. The communion moves toward union of self and other. The tree seems less of a curious "it" and more of an intimate "Thou."

Robert Frost wrote:

The way a crow
Shook down on me
The dust of snow
From a hemlock tree
Has given my heart
A change of mood
And saved some part
Of a day I had rued.3

Frost doesn't address nature as a personified being he can talk to in the second person. The crow, snow and hemlock remain third person objects. But his inner mood is touched by and connected to them in some mysterious yet tangible way.

e. e. cummings wrote of "leaping greenly spirits of trees ... and of love and wings and of gay great happening illimitably earth."[4] Trees and wings and

---

[3] Robert Frost, New Hampshire: A Poem with Notes and Grace Notes (New York: Henry Holt and Co., 1923), p. 82
4 e e cummings, *Xaiper*, (Liveright, 1994)

earth remain in the third person – he's not talking to them. But they feel more like lovers than separate objects. This is union with nature.

The poetry of Mary Oliver and Gary Snyder also point to a sense of union.

One theory says the earth is a complex organism called "Gaia." Gaia isn't a personified being we talk to. It is a third person objective object. Yet we are inside her. Caring for Gaia is caring for us. We aren't so separate. Our fates are deeply connected.

3rd Person Oneness

If we continue to go into this to what Buber calls I-Thou union, it evolves into Oneness or Identification: I-I merging.

I experienced this once as I walked through the woodlands. I noticed a black butterfly in the dusty path. I knelt to see her. Her ragged wings were too weak to lift her into the air. As I watched her abdomen expanding and contracting in labored breath I imagined myself on my deathbed. I knew I, like this butterfly, would die some day. It's our nature to move around in this world and then die. In this we were exactly the same. Yes, our bodies and nervous systems were very different in countless ways. But in the end, she would die and I would die. This was more important than the shape of our limbs. In this most important aspect, we were truly One.

This wasn't a first person perspective with me talking to my inner butterfly. It wasn't a second person perspective with me talking to the external butterfly in any meaningful fashion. It remained fully a third person objective view. And yet, in what was most essential – life passing into death – we weren't separate or even connected. We were poignantly One.

Then the moment passed.

If you've had similar moments, then you've known God, Spirit, Ultimacy or Nature as a third person identification or third person Oneness.

Expanding the Circle

I'll leave it here for today. Next time we'll look at the first and second person perspectives to see how they unfold.

Still, some of you may be asking, "So what? What does this have to do with my daily life?"

I hope this will become obvious as we explore further. We'll see that these perspectives and levels of maturity affect not only how we see God or what's most real in life. They affect how we see anything and everything, including who is in our circle of caring and how we hear one another.

When people intone God or what's fundamental or what's most important and you disagree with them, don't attack their value system or their God. That's usually futile.

Instead, listen deeply to hear their perspective. Are they concerned for the well-being of themselves or family? In other words, are they coming from an internal first person perspective? Are they talking relationally about the importance of love, friendship, caring and civility? Or are they talking externally about how the world works? First, second or third person perspective?

All three are valuable. The internal view emphasizes self-responsibility. The relational view emphasizes how we are held accountable for what we do. And the objective view emphasizes humility and how tiny each of us is in the vast web of life. We need all three in today's world.

Then sense the person's level of development. All levels, including the youngest, have some value. Rather than attack their understanding, appeal to a slightly more inclusive, more mature version of their perspective. That encourages natural unfolding. And it's more likely to succeed.

But first we need to have a good sense of our own view – our own preference. Where do your views of God, nature or reality fall on the matrix map? What are your views maturing toward? What perspective do you bring to the circle of caring?

2. Spiritual Literacy

I've worn glasses for forty-five years. I'm slightly farsighted and have a significant astigmatism in my left eye. Lenses compensate nicely. Looking through them, you and the rest of the world come into clear focus.

But if you tried to look through my glasses, they'd probably make your vision worse. Each of us sees a little differently. What helps one person may give another person a headache.

Ultimate

This is the second sermon in a series on God. By "God" I mean what is ultimately most real or ultimately most important in life.

We can directly experience ultimate reality. Many of us do, if only in moments. But we can't adequately express it in words. Language is limited. Ultimate reality is limitless. The Chinese sage Lao Tsu wrote, "The Tao that can be spoken of is not the eternal Tao; The name that can be named is not the eternal name."[5] Christian mystics use the word "God" to name images and ideas about the ultimate. They use the word "Godhead" to point to the experience beyond images and ideas – the Tao that cannot be named.

In this series, we aren't talking about the actual experience of ultimate reality. We're talking about lenses that help bring that experience into focus.

---

[5] Translation by Ren Jiyu et al. (1993)

All of our minds and hearts have been distorted by our journeys through life. All of us are a bit nearsighted or farsighted or have some kind of astigmatism.

There are many lenses we can look through: God, Allah, Tao, Buddha nature, highest truth, nirvana, enlightenment, the Beloved, nature, the universe.

The words and practices that help our mind-heart may be useless to someone else. And vice versa.

Map

In the last sermon we began to draw a map of all the lenses through which we might view what's most real or most important in life. It has two dimensions: perspective and maturity.

We noted that perspective refers to where we look for God or Spirit. Some people look inside themselves: an internal view. Some look at how they relate to other people or things: a relational view. Some look "out there": an objective view. Ken Wilber[6] calls these first, second and third person perspectives.

As we engage in any of these, it starts to unfold. So the second dimension on the map is maturity. Last time we looked at three developmental levels: separateness, connection and Oneness or merging. Wilber refers to these as communion, union and

---

[6] Ken Wilber, *Integral Spirituality*, (Integral Books: Boston and London), 2007. *One Two Three of God,* audio recording by *Sounds True,* www.soundstrue.come.

2. *Spiritual Literacy*

identification. The Jewish mystic Martin Buber might call them I-it, I-Thou and I-I.

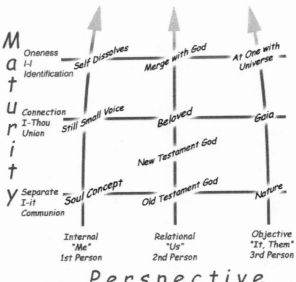

Previously we looked in detail at the unfolding of the third person objective view of nature. Now we'll look at God from relational and internal perspectives and some of the issues that come up around them.

Second Person Relational

In the West, the most familiar images of God are Biblical. These are relational perspectives with God as separate.

In Genesis, the first book of the Old Testament, we find two versions of this God. One is a remote and foreboding Almighty who moves across the face of chaos to divide light from dark, land from ocean and day from night. Jehovah smites people and at least once destroys the world with a flood. The other Old Testament image of God is anthropomorphic: he walks in the Garden of Eden with Adam and Eve in early evenings. Both images are wholly other. We might communicate with Him. But He is very separate.

In the New Testament, Jesus' God is more intimate. Jesus addresses God as "Abba," an Aramaic word similar to "daddy." Jesus' relationship with God is suffused with parent-child love.

Politicians and TV evangelists would have us believe that most Americans subscribe to this view. But Gallop polls tell us that only a small minority (17%) believe in a traditional Biblical God.

Most Unitarian Universalists reject this God as too literal and concrete. I'm reminded of Galileo's inquisitioners. Church doctrine said nothing about moons around Jupiter, so they refused to look through his telescope. We wish they would have.

The Biblical view of God is just a lens. Rather than critique it, why not take a peek? Why not suspend our skepticism and try to engage in a sincere conversation with the Ultimate and see what happens?

One of the easiest ways to relate to God is to sing to God.

I was introduced to Hindu and Sufi chanting back in the days when I was a hard-core scientific-materialistic atheist who had little patience with God language. Yet I loved to sing these simple songs the same way many of you love to sing

Amazing Grace even if you don't agree with the theology.

I invite you to indulge me and join in a devotional song. It uses the phrase "Lord of Light" to speak with a being "out there."

Some of you will find it easy to give yourself to the singing. Some of you may hesitate. But don't worry. You'll be fine. It won't cause permanent damage, I promise.

> *O take a hand, take a hand Lord of Light.*
> *And make us whole again.*
> *O take a hand my Lord of Light,*
> *And make us whole again,*
> *And make us whole again.*

We humans are intensely relational creatures. We can't survive without others. Relational instincts are deeply wired into us. Rather than fight them, these practices use them as a tool to bring us into a more intimate relationship with ultimate reality. If we engage these practices sincerely, our consciousness may gradually shift in several ways.

First, our hearts open. These are heart-centered practices. Devotion is not about what the mind thinks. It's about what the heart feels. Our sense of love broadens and deepens. It becomes less sentimentally attached to a few particular people or things and more dispassionately embracing of all life.

With this, our sense of who or what we're singing to or communicating with becomes more immediate. The 15th century ecstatic poet Kabir wrote, "I laugh when I hear the fish in the water is thirsty."[7] God is an ocean and we're inside it.

A Sufi chant sings "Ishk Allah ma bood leh la" or "God is the lover, the beloved and love itself." The distinction between us and Abba, between us and ultimacy, begins to come together in union.

If we carry these practices with us all the time, the sense of who or what is singing or praying starts to thin out. Rumi wrote: "It is said that love comes through a window in the heart, but if there are no walls, there's no need to have a window." This is merging with the Light, becoming One with the unnamable All.

We've risen from separateness through connection to merging. It's not an intellectual thing but a heartful movement from communion to union to identification.

Right before we disappear off the top of the map into the direct experience of the Tao or the Godhead, there's still a wisp of lover and beloved. But it's not the same God or Spirit of Life found in the younger levels.

First Person Internal

Now, turning from the relational perspective to the first person internal perspective, we find a similar movement. However, this perspective emphasizes the mind rather than the heart, what we see more than what we feel.

---

[7] Robert Bly, *The Kabir Book: Forty-Four of the Ecstatic Poems of Kabir,* (Beacon Press, Boston, 1977), p. 9

Imagine a person coming across a book describing the God within: the inner light, Atman, soul essence. "What a great idea," she thinks. "I like the thought of a divine essence in me."

This is an internal separate view. It's internal because it's inside her and it's separate because, despite her enthusiasm, it's just an idea, not an experience.

Nevertheless, it may be enough to get her to examine her deep experience. Maybe she takes up meditation. She senses stirrings within she hadn't noticed before – subtle but tangible.

She's rising from separateness to connection, from communion to union. Kabir sometimes wrote with the voice of a first person union God:

... You will not find me in stupas, not in Indian shrine rooms, nor in synagogues, nor in cathedrals:

not in masses, nor kirtans, not in legs winding around your own neck, nor in eating nothing but vegetables.

*When you really look for me, you will see me instantly
you will find me in the tiniest house of time.*

Kabir says: Student, tell me, what is God?

He is the breath inside the breath.[8]

"The breath inside the breath," is an internal, connected view. One time Kabir put it more simply: "The God whom I love is inside." Quakers refer to this as "the still small voice within."

---

[8] Robert Bly, op. cit. p. 33

If she continues to explore this still small place within, it may not seem so small. The clarity, peace and love inside grow stronger until she, the observer, begins to dissolve into this inner quiet.

Kabir writes, "Because someone has made up the word 'wave,' do I have to distinguish it from water?"

The merging of the wave with the ocean is similar in all three perspectives, but has slightly different flavors.

From the third person objective perspective we see the immensity of the ocean of existence. We're a tiny, single wave. But we're part of it all nonetheless. We're at One with the universe.

From the second person relational perspective, the ocean is vast but our relationship with it feels more intimate and personal. We merge with God.

From the first person internal perspective, we know we're a wave, but our essence is the same as the ocean. As our awareness moves from the shape of our wave to the ocean, our self-sense dissolves.

All three ultimately point to the same experience. Yet because of the limitations of language, anything we say has the flavor of one of the three perspectives.

"At One with the universe," "merging with God," "self dissolving" are just lenses. Ultimate experience is beyond perspective and beyond language. The Tao that can be spoken isn't the true Tao.

Art, Ethics and Science

If we step back from all these levels and perspectives and look at the whole map, we notice that religion in the West got a little stuck on the relational separate view. I'd like to put this into a historical context and hint at the implications it has for the human condition in the twenty-first century.

Remember, these three perspectives are different realms of human experience. As noted last Sunday, art is the internal realm: how something touches us inside. Art is in the eye (or "I") of the beholder. Morals and ethics are in the relational realm: how we treat one another. And science is in the objective realm – a scientist takes an impersonal external view.

Through the late medieval period, arts, ethics and science were fused. They weren't well differentiated. Art was restricted to religious themes. Morality was based on Biblical injunctions. Scientific findings had to be reconciled with church doctrine or be rejected.

The Western Enlightenment began about 400 years ago in the time of Galileo. Its great accomplishment was the separation of these three realms so each had its own dignity and could stand on its own apart from the church.[9]

Artists began to paint non-religious themes: landscapes, still-lifes and everyday scenes. Philosophers began to think about ethics outside

---

[9] Ken Wilber, *The Marriage of Sense and Soul,* (Random House, New York, 1998)

the confines of church teaching – they called it "natural philosophy." Scientific discoveries were seen as legitimate whether the church approved or not.

Freed from the yoke of the church, science took off. It made staggering advances in astronomy, physics, medicine, food production, transportation, communication, technologies and on and on. It extended life expectancy by several decades.

Science was so successful that it began to dominate the way people thought. Its third person objective perspective became more than just *A* way to view life. It became *THE* way. Objectivity was in. Internal and relational views were passé.

As one philosopher put it, before the Western Enlightenment, to be caught on your knees praying was a sign of maturity, dignity and wisdom. After the Enlightenment era, to be caught on your knees praying was an embarrassment and sign that you were quaint, old fashioned and out of touch with modern sensibilities.

Disaster

While the Enlightenment's scientific achievements improved the human condition in many ways, in other ways it was a disaster.

Science knows little about values. Morals and values come from the relational realm. Science gets its strength from being objective and value-free. Science can tell us a great deal about the difference between a pine tree, spotted owl, yellow-tailed butterfly and comet. But it can't tell us which is better or worse, more valuable or less valuable.

Instinctively, we know love is better than hate and generosity is better than selfishness. But science shows us nothing of these.

Meanwhile, the traditional church remained stuck in a relational perspective, and a relatively young level.

Karen Armstrong, a popularizer of Biblical scholarship, noted that most people first learn about God around the same time they first learn about Santa Claus.[10] After all, both are bearded gentlemen with loving and kind intentions.

This lens on God isn't bad or wrong. It portrays a loving, welcoming universe. It encourages kindness and thoughtfulness. It's appropriate for the concrete, literal thinking of a child. But for the nuanced complexities of an inquisitive adult mind, it's a little goofy.

So our view of Santa Claus evolves as we grow. Unfortunately, for many people the word "God" remains stunted in a mythic consciousness appropriate for a seven year old.

There are many exceptions to this. Many people have matured beyond this.

Still, if we meet a stranger on the commuter train and he uses the word "God," our first assumption may be that he was talking about an infinitely perfect Santa Claus. This is too bad.

As I noted earlier, only 17% of Americans actually subscribe to a literal Biblical God. Most

---

[10] Karen Armstrong, *The Case for God*, (Alfred A. Knof, New York, 2009), p 320.

have more rational, pluralistic and connected ways of thinking.

However when it comes to public discourse on religion or values, the West is developmentally arrested. We don't have a shared vocabulary, set of tools or institutional support for these discussions because they can't be couched in objective scientific thinking and popular religion remains mired in young relational ways of thinking.

Unitarianism

Unitarianism is one of the many exceptions to the general trend. For four hundred years we've insisted on pluralistic thinking, inclusion, diversity and seeing things from multiple perspectives. Our banners around the sanctuary and symbols in other Unitarian Universalist congregations declare that there are many valuable lenses through which to view ultimacy.

Nevertheless, we have our quirks. Many feel betrayed by the limitations of the traditional church. Sometimes we throw out the baby with the bathwater. In rejecting those limitations we sometimes reject the entire second person perspective as a legitimate place from which to grow and evolve. Some of us are wary of God language.

Group-Centric Consciousness

Next time I want to pick up here and look at where we are today. There is a level of consciousness that has matured beyond separateness but hasn't fully found connection. It connects with some people but not all people. It identifies strongly with one group, religious brand, ethnicity or nation and treats others as unworthy of care or concern. It accepts one set of values passed down from some higher source and treats others as a threat.

This consciousness breeds most of the world's terrorism. It's the source of take-no-prisoners politics and "I know how to run the country and anyone who disagrees is in the way." It arguably contributed to our economic melt down two years ago as well as to the assault on public education, health care, environmental sensitivity and so forth.

If we want to be a force for healing in the world, we need to address more than just individual issues. We must help this consciousness mature.

Spiritual Literacy

To be spiritually literate, we must be fluent in all perspectives and all levels without confusing them. To enrich our lives and be in meaningful dialog with the world, we need to be able to converse clearly and compassionately in all perspectives and at all levels. And we need to encourage ourselves and others to mature toward higher levels rather than defend where we or they are now.

If we can find ourselves on the map of consciousness, we still have more to grow. The Tao that can be thought is not the true Tao. Any concept of God is just a lens, not ultimate reality. Any view that isn't imbued with our ultimate potential misses some internal beauty, relational goodness or objective clarity.

3. Consciousness

An ancient Sufi story tells of two men looking at the sky one clear evening. One remarks on how beautiful the two moons are. The other says, "Two moons? My friend, there is only one moon. You must be seeing double."

The first replies, "Nonsense. If I were seeing double there'd be four moons."

Consciousness

Consciousness is the way we process information and assign meaning to it. We take for granted that what we see is real. Yet all we perceive or remember passes through the lenses of our consciousness. These lenses can easily make us see double or distort in other ways.

This is the third sermon in a series about God. In the next talk we'll simply and directly answer the question, "Does God exist?" However, before we can do this we have to know which consciousness is asking the question – which lens we use to view the topic.

So in this talk I'd like to explore consciousness and how it changes as we mature individually and evolve as a species. Before we look at these stages, there are five things to know about consciousness in general.

1. Affects Everything

Consciousness affects everything we experience. Since it's how we process information and assign meaning, it affects how we see ourselves, our relationships and the world. It affects our values, how we treat our families, organize society, think of the oppressed, decide to go to war, view the national budget, relate to the environment and every other aspect of life, including how we see or don't see God.

2. Unaware

Though consciousness affects everything, paradoxically we're mostly unaware of it. Like the man seeing double, we pay little attention to our lenses of consciousness. I wear glasses. It's amazing how fuzzy and blurry the world can become before it occurs to me that my glasses might be dirty. We're usually unaware of our consciousness.

3. Stages

Consciousness matures in stages. We have to master one stage before we can grow into the next because each stage has the building blocks for the next. Each stage transcends the previous by going beyond its limits. And it includes the previous by incorporating it into a higher synthesis.[11]

For example, we have to crawl before we can walk and walk before we can run.

We have to read letters before we can read words, read words before we can read sentences and read sentences before we can read a book. The skills unfold in natural stages.

---

[11] Ken Wilber uses the phrase "transcend and include."

4. Radical Shifts

Even though the stages of consciousness unfold naturally from each other, the world and the meanings we assign to it look radically different through different consciousnesses.

The world we know crawling around the house is different from the world we discover running through streets and fields. The world we know as runners includes the world of crawling. But it's so different that it's impossible to adequately describe it to someone who can only crawl.

The depth, texture, nuances and meaning of a book is unimaginable when we can only read single words.

5. Multiple Consciousness

We live in multiple stages. Our consciousness can be advanced in one area and young in another. We can be an advanced reader and unable to walk. We can be an athletic runner and illiterate. We can be an intellectual genius and a social nincompoop. We can be a political savant and an ethical idiot.

Stages

Let's turn from consciousness in general to specific stages. In talking about God or Spirit in earlier sermons, I differentiated three stages: separateness, connection and merging. They unfold in this order. We have to know self and spirit as separate before we know how they connect. We have to know connection before we can know merging.

This sequence may not be intuitively obvious because these are big leaps. Therefore, rather than just three stages, let's differentiate six. We could easily differentiate eight, nine or twelve. But six may be enough to see the developmental spectrum clearly.

As we do this, we'll take a quick look at six views of Jesus. Christians around the world think about Jesus through the lenses of their consciousness. So let's note these various portraits of Jesus as they relate to maturity of consciousness.

Stages of Consciousness[12]			
	World View	**Thinking**	**Jesus as**
Tribal	Pre-Self	Magical	Magician
Ancient	Self-centric	Mythical	Hero-Savior
Traditional	Group-centric	Literal	Law Giver
Modern	World-centric	Rational	Tradition Breaker
Postmodern	Pluralistic	Pluralistic	Humanitarian
Integral	Universal	Trans-rational	Cosmic Consciousness

Tribal Pre-Self

We'll start with tribal consciousness. It has no sense of self as we understand it today. Traditional tribal people draw identity from the group and its customs and traditions: "We hunt in the valley and not in the mountains because that is the way of the

---

[12] This table has been drawn and adapted from the work of Ken Wilber, op. cit. and Don Beck and Christopher Cowan, *Spiral Dynamics,* (Blackwell Publishing, 2006)

ancestors." Even the tribal chief is strictly bound by tradition. Tribal gods are powerful and arbitrary.

Tribal thinking is magical by scientific standards – it understands there are causes and effects but does not understand the mechanisms.

We all grow through this stage of thinking as children. I remember when my brother told me, "Step on a crack and you break your mother's back." I worried whether "cracks" included the straight lines in the sidewalk or just the jagged breaks. I also searched for four leaf clovers and avoided walking under ladders.

Adults capable of rational thought may still hold magical beliefs about God, economics or other aspects of life.

Examples of tribal thinking include street gangs, athletic team bonding, good luck charms, family feuds and heavy reliance on rites and rituals. Another example is Jesus the magician who turned water into wine, walked across the waves, fed thousands from seven loaves of bread and raised Lazarus from the dead.

Ancient Self-Centrism

The problem with tribal consciousness is its inflexibility. So about 10,000 years ago a new, self-centric consciousness emerged. Maybe there was a famine. Someone left the traditional hunting grounds and killed an animal in the sacred mountains. He was frightened that the ancestral gods would punish him. Yet, he became strong and well nourished while others remained weak and dying.

Rather than being totally bound by tradition, he followed personal instincts and intelligence. And he thrived. His self-sense began to differentiate from the tribal whole. It was exciting and empowering. If the tribe didn't expel him, it may have made him a shaman.

Self-centric thinking is called "mythic" because it has a grandiose sense of power. It can be creative and adventurous. Examples include the terrible twos, adventurous youth, wild rock stars, villains in James Bond movies, frontier mentality, Achilles in Homer's Iliad, Attila the Hun, Libya's Muammar Gaddafi and in his followers' hero worship of him.

Another example is Jesus the hero-savior who, through heroic sacrifice, saves us from eternal torment if we just have faith in him.

About 20% of the world and about 5% of its leaders see through a mythic, self-centric lens.[13]

Traditional Group-Centrism

The problem with self-centrism is the harm it visits on those around it. So about 5,000 years ago, group-centrism emerged.

Following a mythic hero or avoiding a mythic villain left both supporters and victims in a bad way. Self-centric heroes keep most of the bounty, leaving everyone else empty-handed. So rather than just kill them and take their place, some people began to think about others in their group. To fairly distribute food, clothing, justice and care for the

---

[13] Ken Wilber, op. cit. and Don Beck and Christopher Cowan, op. cit.

3. *Consciousness*

weak, they began to live by group rules rather than one leader's whim.

Group-centric consciousness emphasizes laws passed down from higher authority. Those who value these laws and customs are "us." Those who don't are "them." This consciousness connects with some people, but not all people. It emphasizes meaning, direction, purpose, order, authority and moralistic teaching.

Its thinking is literal and concrete. It's more logical than impulsive egotism. Yet it isn't fully rational. It's typical of pre-adolescent children.

Examples in adults include ethnocentrism, love-it-or-leave it patriotism, fundamentalism of all stripes, Paul Ryan's budget, economic policies that confuse the good of the whole with the good of the wealthy few, the Tea Party, Lake Woebegone, codes of chivalry, Confucian China, "traditional values" and politicians who believe that anyone who disagrees with them is an enemy to defeat rather than a fellow citizen to work with.

Another example is Jesus the lawgiver and embodiment of eternal truth. Some of his laws were "do unto others as you would have them do unto you" and "love your neighbor." Applying these laws to everyone is wonderful. But ethnocentrism applies them to the faithful while condemning or at best ignoring everyone else.

This consciousness includes 30% of world leaders, 40% of the population, 70% of organized religion and over 95% of terrorist groups.[14]

---

[14] Ken Wilber op. cit. and Beck and Cowen, op. cit.

To be sure, there are lone, egocentric terrorists. But they have trouble organizing others because they aren't group-centered. Ethnocentric people do more serious damage worldwide. Those not adhering to their values are seen as threats deserving to be blown up. And they have the organizational ability to pull it off.

This group-centric lens is a natural stage of consciousness we all grow through. But when people get stuck in this pre-adolescence, it's bad news. It perpetrates violence. It tries to destroy social programs, environmental protection, public education and anything else that supports everyone rather than just their group.

Many people who have higher pluralistic or integral thinking still have ethnocentric values and beliefs. They use their higher functioning in service of concrete, literal and pre-rational goals. This is bad news.

Modern World-Centrism

About five hundred years ago, a new world-centric consciousness emerged. It's called "world-centric" because it takes into account those outside its group.

World-centric people are capable of full rationality. They can view their and other's beliefs objectively. That is the heart of rationality – genuine objective observation.

World-centrism emphasizes creativity, personal expression, innovation, breaking tradition, entrepreneurial spirit, prosperity now, mobility, nimbleness and understanding systems. It's individualism as understood in the modern world.

A fully rational, world-centric person is unlikely to blow somebody up. He may hire someone to do dirty tricks for him but is less likely to hire an assassin.

Examples of World-centrism include the Western Enlightenment, emerging middle class, scientific revolution, industrial revolution, Wall Street, the advertising industry, the Cold War and chambers of commerce when they often pursue their goals without adequately taking into account the larger good.

Another example of world-centrism is Jesus the tradition breaker. He threw moneychangers out of the temple. When asked about the law requiring stoning of an adulteress, he famously said, "He who has never sinned can cast the first stone." When asked to condemn a woman who broke the Sabbath to care for her son, he refused. He appealed to something deeper and higher than literal interpretations of the old laws.

This lens of consciousness accounts for 30% of the world's population, about 15% of leaders and the majority of Americans.[15]

Post-Modern Pluralism

Rationality, the Western Enlightenment, science and world-centric thinking have done great things for humanity. But they have a dark side. Think of

---

[15] Beck and Cowen, op. cit. and Ken Wilber, *One Two Three of God*, op. cit.

the damage some large corporations wreck and you'll have a feel for the dark side of world-centrism: materialism, eco-destruction, unequal wealth distribution, tyranny of the most ambitious, corporate personhood, and so forth. World-centrism is aware of other people, values and beliefs but puts its own interests above the larger good. Group-centric people have little understanding of those outside their group. World-centric people understand others enough to manipulate them for personal advantage.

So about 50 years ago a new pluralist consciousness emerged and transcended these weaknesses. It not only understood others, but valued them. It put the welfare of others on an equal footing with self-care – and sometimes made it more important.

Pluralism values multiculturalism, group harmony, inner peace, equity, caring for the oppressed, good communication and including everyone.

Examples include ACLU, Doctors without Borders, Jimmy Carter's human rights efforts, animal rights, Jacques Cousteau, Deep Ecology, the original Ben & Jerry's, John Lennon, sensitivity training, feminism and the Civil Rights movement.

It also includes Unitarian Universalism. We have people who are group-centric, rational and integral. However pluralism is our center of gravity: the inherent worth and dignity of every person, the goodness of everyone, openness, curiosity, love and respect for the interdependent web.

Another example is Jesus the Humanitarian. He looked out for the poor and the oppressed. His parable of the Good Samaritan illustrated how people we don't like can be good. He encouraged loving our enemies.

Pluralistic Christians say, "Jesus taught us to love our neighbors and care for others. So did Buddha, Gandhi and other great teachers. They're all valuable, but I call myself 'Christian' because Jesus resonates with me. He's my guy. He's not better than others, just what works best in my heart."

Pluralism accounts for about 10% of the world population and 15% of those in power.[16]

Integral Transrational

We Unitarian Universalist might like to think that we're the top of the heap – the most evolved. But not so. Pluralistic and Unitarian Universalist consciousness has a dark side. Trying to include everyone can break down into tokenism. Desire to help the oppressed can breed competition to see who is most oppressed. Compassion can give without asking for anything in return and become paternalistic or patronizing. Fair representation can give equal weight to the informed and the uninformed alike. Discomfort with judging can lead to lack of discernment. Seeing goodness in everyone can lead to not holding people accountable. Emphasis on feelings can lead to the tyranny of the

---

[16] Beck and Cowen, op. cit., and Ken Wilber, op. cit.

most disgruntled – those with the strongest feelings sway the group.

So in the last few decades, higher more sophisticated stages of consciousness have emerged. They've been called "integral," "vision logic," "trans-rational," "holistic" and "overmind." Examples include the work of Ken Wilber, Stephen Hawking and chaos theory.

Another example is Jesus as cosmic consciousness. This images sees Jesus as a self-realized being who showed us a path to our emerging divinity. Such a Christian feels this Christ consciousness inside him or herself and sees it in others. Jesus was an inspiring expression – nothing more and nothing less.

Second Tier

Researchers studying the development of intelligence, morals, worldviews, self-identity, values and more note that the shift to Integral is huge. It's so large that many call the stages from tribalism to pluralism "first tier" and integral the beginning of "second tier" consciousness.[17]

To understand this shift it helps to remember that consciousness is the way we process information and assign meaning.

For example, the word "Jesus" has information but no inherent meaning – it's just sound waves or marks on a page. But the mind assigns meaning. We've noted six different meanings: powerful

---

[17] Beck and Cowen, op. cit., and Ken Wilber, op. cit.

3. *Consciousness*

magician, hero-savior, law bringer, tradition breaker, humanitarian and Christ consciousness.

The word "God" has a greater variety of meanings, all assigned by the mind. The word "Obamacare" has no inherent meaning. Even the laws and policies have no inherent meaning. So different people assign it different meanings: "caring," "socialism," "rectifying a social inequity," "government sticking its nose where it doesn't belong," and more.

Each stage of consciousness is a characteristic way we process information and assign meaning to it.

People in first tier consciousness cannot understand people in stages other than their own. Pluralistic progressives think group-centric conservatives are throwbacks to the Dark Ages. Self-centric Tea Partiers think liberals have drifted into outer space. Democrats and Republicans may deem the others have lost their marbles: "I don't understand how they think!"

In the first tier, people tend to think those in their own stage are reasonable, those in earlier stages are idiots and those in higher stages aren't living in the real world. If you've ever asked, "How could they think that way!" you're probably referring to someone in a different stage of consciousness than yours.

Integral consciousness is the first stage complex enough to see another stage and genuinely "get it." It's called "integral" because it can comprehend and value all the lower stages at once. It can talk with someone at a different level without being condescending and without losing its own higher perspective.

For example, let's say we're promoting an environmental policy with a factory owner. We recognize that he's ethnocentric – he cares about his family, his job, his industry and has little patience with others. If we're integral thinkers, we won't talk to him about how much better we'll all feel if we care about everyone – a pluralist, Unitarian Universalist value. We talk about ethnocentric values and how this policy will help his group. And we do this genuinely and sincerely because we know he's not stupid – just looking through a different consciousness. We aren't being manipulative because the reasons we give him are sincere and complete within his frame of consciousness.

In the World

Understanding all these stages of consciousness is complex. Nevertheless, in today's world we face many complex problems all at once. Most have roots in these stages of consciousness. If there were no adults stuck in group-centric consciousness or below we wouldn't have ethnocentrism, homophobia, the war in Iraq, the financial meltdown of 2008, the Israeli-Palestinian struggle, large-scale terrorism or Paul Ryan's draconic budget. If there were no adults stuck in world-centric consciousness or below we wouldn't have global warming, political gridlock or predatory corporations.

Consciousness is how we process information, assign meaning and create narratives. It determines the problems we see or don't see, the problems we create or solve and what we tell each other about them.

Pluralistic consciousness – the heart of Unitarian Universalism – is complex enough to see the problems in the world and feel bad about them. It can address them one at a time. But it isn't complex enough to see the patterns of consciousness, information processing and meaning assignment underlying them. First tier stages have difficulty seeing outside their own perspectives.

Most people with advanced college degrees have used integral consciousness at least intellectually. Almost all Unitarian Universalists are intellectually capable of integral thinking. [18] However we don't necessarily have integral values, beliefs, social organization, politics, self-identity, worldview and so forth. But we have the capacity.

Bootstrap

How do we bootstrap ourselves into integral consciousness?

This is a large topic for another time. So I'll just hint at two areas to consider:

1. We can help each other by talking deeply with one another about values, beliefs, worldview, self-identity and so forth. We can use our intellectual

---

[18] Among those involved in organized religions, Unitarian Universalists are, on average, among the highest educated. To get those degrees, they've had to use integral thinking. Those who don't have advanced degrees are probably capable of integral integral thinking as well or they won't be comfortable in our religious communities.

integral capacities in conversations to help us mature in other areas.

2. We can help ourselves through serious spiritual practice. These help break down consciousness structures over time and allow them to gradually integrate at higher stages.

Happiness

Finally, there are different textures to happiness and well being in each stage. Integral happiness is lighter and more selfless than earlier stages. It is less dependent on people or things being a specific way. This makes it more stable and resilient.

May we all know higher forms of happiness, for ourselves and for the world.

4. Real?

Is God real?

We've been exploring the lenses through which people look at what is ultimately most real or ultimately most important in life. We've looked at various perspectives and levels of maturity. We've created maps of these points of view.

It's time we cut to the chase and ask, "Is God Real? Doug, what do you believe? Does God exist or not?"

Unitarian Universalist that I am, I want to hedge by asking, "What do you mean by 'God'?" And I'll do a lot of hedging in a moment. But first I owe you a simple, straight answer. Taking it as a serious question, using my own deepest understanding I would say, "Yes, God is real."

I arrive at this answer in two ways. One is to say God is "phenomenologically real." This a good Unitarian Universalist answer. It's convincing but not very satisfying. Two is to say God is "absolutely real." This isn't so convincing but ultimately more satisfying.[19]

In each case, the answer is "yes." And each way of arriving at the answer has value. So let's unpack it each way – hopefully without hedging too much.

---

[19] Ken Wilber, *The One Two Three of God*, op. cit.

Phenomenologically Real

To say God is phenomenologically real means there are real phenomena that people experience and these phenomena have measureable effects.

To explore this, let's go back to our map of the lenses through which we view God. Here's a version that includes most of what we've explored so far:

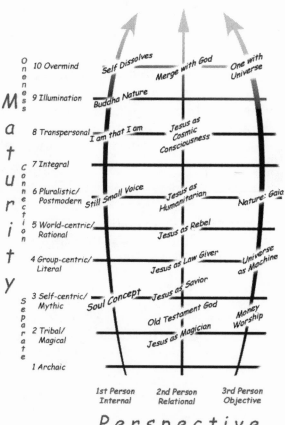

There are three basic perspectives on God or three places where people look for God. The first person perspective looks inside. It emphasizes practices like meditation and contemplation. The second person perspective looks at how we relate to one another or to life in general. It emphasizes devotion and surrender and practices like prayer and chanting. The third person perspective looks for God objectively in the external world. It emphasizes rationality, inquiry, scientific methodology and observation.

Reality includes all three perspectives. So all three are legitimate. We may personally prefer one to another. That's fine. Yet each is completely valid. Therefore our map includes all three along its horizontal dimension.

The vertical dimension is maturity. As we engage with any perspective, it unfolds developmentally. Some views are appropriate for a child or novice. Others are appropriate for an adult or spiritual master. In the first two sermons we looked at three points in this developmental spectrum: separation, connection and merging or oneness.

In the third sermon, we broke down this developmental spectrum into six smaller steps: tribal/magic, self-centric/ mythic, group-centric/literal, world-centric/rational, pluralistic/postmodern and integral.

These six stages outline the most familiar areas in the developmental spectrum. To be more complete, we could add an archaic stage before tribal and several stages beyond integral: "transpersonal," "illumination" and "overmind."

It's hard to describe these higher stages because so few people achieve them that we don't have much data about them. And the data we have can be fully understood only by those who've gotten there.[20]

But for our purposes, it's enough to note that there are stages beyond integral. These include the experience of self dissolving, merging with God and oneness with the universe.

This gives us three perspectives and ten developmental stages or thirty different lenses through which to view God, Spirit, ultimate reality or what's ultimately most important in life. The philosopher Ken Wilber refers to these as cosmic addresses.[21] They can be fun to play with.

For example, consider the God who walked in the Garden of Eden with Adam and Eve. This is a relational perspective and a mythic consciousness. Its address is 2nd person, level 3. Or simply a 2-3 god.

In Exodus 3:14: "God said to Moses, I AM THAT I AM: and he said, Thus shall you say to the children of Israel, I AM has sent me to you." What kind of God is described as "I am that I am"? ... It sounds 1st person transpersonal level 8. Its cosmic address on our map might be 1-8.

---

[20] For example Stephen Hawking's *Brief History of Time*, David Bohm's theories, Teihard de Chardin, Aurobindo, Ken Wilber's spectrum of consciousness.
[21] Ken Wilber op. cit.

Or maybe we see nature as what's ultimately most real. Walking in the wilderness we feel connected with the forests and mountains. Maybe this isn't exactly a feeling of Oneness but is a personal emotional bond to nature as Gaia. This is a 3rd person perspective with a pluralistic consciousness or a 3-6 view of Spirit.

As long as we are considering traditional images of God, we might look at less traditional. Let's say a person views money as what's ultimately most important in her life – the primary organizing factor. It's her functional equivalent of God. This is an objective view (money is an external object) and it's rather young: a magical or mythical object. So the Golden Calf's address might be 3-2.5.

To be sure we have these addresses correct, we'd have to listen carefully to the way a person describes God or Spirit or reality.

The point is that we can look at any place on the map and find people – probably large groups of people – for whom a God at that address is phenomenologically real. They believe in a God in that vicinity. They feel it in their guts or in their hearts. It affects how they treat other people and how they organize their lives. It has tangible impacts. It's phenomenologically real.

Objection

Someone might object to this line of reasoning saying, "My God is real because I experience a still small voice within. His God is unreal because it's anthropomorphic – an infinitely perfect Santa Claus. Mine is authentic. His is ridiculous."

To this we could say, "Well, the white haired, loving gentleman in the clouds may be a young image of God – a 2nd person mythic or a 2-3 god. But it has some truth even if it's a little silly. Your still small voice is more sophisticated – 1st person pluralistic or a 1-6 image. But there are views on God more mature than yours. From those higher stages, yours looks naïve. So why should we accept yours but not his? They're each real to one of you."

Rather than get into my-God-is-better-than-your-God fights, we can acknowledge that each represents genuine experience that has meaningful impacts.

As Unitarian Universalists seeped in pluralistic, post-modern values, we affirm and support everyone's search for truth and meaning and the legitimacy of many views of ultimate reality. The banners around this sanctuary convey this broad embrace.

Not Satisfying

Even if this line of thought is compelling, it's not satisfying. Just because somebody fervently believes something doesn't mean it's really true. President Bush convinced Congress and most Americans that Saddam Hussein had weapons of mass destruction. That belief cost thousands of lives, over a trillions dollars, damaged our international standing and helped wreck the economy – it had very real effects. It was phenomenologically real. But Hussein had no weapons. It wasn't true ultimately.

Just because someone feels a personal Biblical version of God in their heart doesn't mean they interpret their experience accurately. Just because we fervently believe that the voice of intuition arising in our hearts has a divine source, that doesn't prove we aren't quietly hallucinating.

Ultimately Real

This brings us to the second way of asking the question: "Is God ultimately real? Is God *really* for real?"

I think it is safe to assume that all the lower developmental addresses of God aren't ultimately real. They may be relatively real. They may contain some truth. But they're not completely real. The Easter Bunny and Tooth Fairy may excite wonder in a child without being completely real.

But what about these upper level Gods? Are they real? And who is even in a position to answer?

The only people who can answer about the higher levels are those who have mastered those stages of consciousness – saints, meditation masters, yogis, evolved scientists and people in ordinary lives who exhibit complex thinking and intuition at the highest levels we can detect.

Researchers have developed ways to identify those few people who may have achieved these higher stages. When asked, "Is God real?" they say "Yes." At least most do – over 90% answer affirmatively.[22]

---

[22] Ken Wilber, *The One Two Three of God* interview op. cit.

What it Means in 1st Person

To understand their answers, we have to look beyond a simple "yes" or "no" and ask them to elaborate on what they mean. This can be tricky.

For example, if we ask most highly trained Buddhists, "Is God real?" they'll say "No" at first. For them the word "God" implies a supernatural being or force outside the world who is pulling strings, influencing evolution, controlling events or giving advice. Buddhists see ultimate reality as interdependent: everything depends on everything else. They see no divine being or force "outside," just natural laws within the interdependent web.

So initially they say, "No."

But if we asked them to elaborate on what they experience, their answer is not as simple as "yes" or "no."

As the mind-heart becomes deeply relaxed, it becomes peaceful and serene. It's empty of thought. It's void of concepts. But the emptiness isn't like walking into a gigantic deep freeze with the lights turned out. The void is not a cold, dark nothingness. Quite the opposite.

Without the swirl of thoughts, the mind is clear, insightful, wise and intelligent. The wise person is not lost in a jungle of thinking. She can calmly see to the heart of a situation. She can see through us.

Without that swirl of thoughts, the heart is filled with love. After all, judgments are thoughts. The quiet heart is more discerning and less judgmental.

4. Real?

It feels weird at first. We think wisdom means being smart about something. But higher wisdom is a *way* of seeing, not *something* that is seen. We think of love as *attached* to a beloved person or object. But this is love *without an object* – just love as a natural state.

The state feels warm and luminous, not cold and dark. A sense of self becomes irrelevant. It dissolves into clarity, kindness and compassion.

If we ask someone deeply familiar with these higher stages, "Does God exist?" what are they going to say?

Two and a half millennia ago when the Buddha was asked, he refused to answer. Saying "yes" would have been misleading, implying a supernatural being or force apart from everything else. And saying "no" would have also been misleading, implying the absence of these divine qualities that permeate the mind-heart when it resists nothing.

So the Buddha remained silent.

Today, when researchers ask people highly developed in first person practices like meditation, "Is God real?" they might say "No," meaning they see nothing supernatural. Or they might say, "Yes," meaning "Existence is inherently alive, joyful, clear, intelligent, wise and luminous."

Statistically, most say "yes." But the Spirit they refer to is very different from the traditional, separate God. Very different. But very real.

What it Means in 3rd Person

Now, let's step back and come at the question, "Is God real?" from a different perspective – the third person perspective. This emphasizes objectivity, inquiry, scientific methodology and clear-headedness.

Complexity

When we look at the universe this way, it's clear that it's creative. The universe moves toward greater and greater complexity. Think about it.

Thirteen billion years ago (give or take a billion) the universe was vastly simpler – a "singularity" in which all matter and energy were crushed down to a small, incredibly dense sameness.

Then it exploded – the "big bang." One instant there was absolute sameness. The next, the universe was expanding and populated by gazillions of sub-atomic particles – simple but not quite as simple as a moment before.

As it expanded and cooled, subatomic particles stuck together creating atomic particles – protons, electrons, neutrons.

As it expanded and cooled more, atomic particles clumped together into hydrogen atoms. The universe was still simple, but not quite so simple.

After a while the clouds of hydrogen compacted into stars. In these infernos, the hydrogen atoms were driven together forming more complex elements: helium, carbon, nitrogen, oxygen and heavier elements like uranium and plutonium.

The stars exploded and scattered these complex elements around the universe. This stuff eventually formed planets.

Our planet was formed some four and a half billion years ago, give or take. The stuff of our planet mixed and mingled, mingled and mixed creating different compounds with different properties. Eventually there were compounds that could replicate themselves – nucleic and amino acids perhaps. These first hints of life were incredibly simple by today's standards.

You know how the story goes: they evolved into single cell organisms, multi-celled organisms, organisms made of tissues and organs. Eventually neural networks evolved. Recently these neural networks became complex enough to be self-aware.

We humans are massive, complex, partially self-aware organisms with more intricacy than we can fathom. And if we think we are the end of the line – the highest of the highest – that is just narcissistic indulgence. All the signs indicate that the universe is just getting started: humans are less than a whistle stop in evolving complexity.

This plot line shows our universe isn't dead matter and energy running down hill. It moves creatively toward greater complexity. This is what we see objectively.

Simplicity

At the same time, another movement runs in the opposite direction – a movement toward simplicity. Rot, decay, death and destruction move from complexity toward simplicity. Everything dies.

Everything put together sooner or later falls apart. Nothing last. Entropy happens. Everything tends to break down into simpler states.

Steadfastness

There's also a third quality called "inertia." At least in the short run, things tend to stay the same. If I place a pencil on this pulpit, it stays where I left it unless some outside force acts upon it.

Brahma, Vishnu, Shiva

These are three fundamental trends: complexity, simplicity and inertia. Creativity, destruction and steadfastness.

In Hinduism these are called Brahma, Vishnu and Shiva. Brahma is the creative. Vishnu is the sustaining. Shiva is the destructive.

In monotheism we have "God the father, creator of heaven and earth and of all things visible and invisible." We have God the sustainer, "who makes me lie down in green pastures [and] leads me beside still waters … Thy rod and Thy staff, they comfort me." (Psalm 23-2,4) And we have Jehovah the wrathful destroyer who wiped out the whole world and sends people to burn in hell.

But from the objective perspective, these are not supernatural forces. They're just properties of the natural universe. They're like gravity. I have no idea why gravity works – why objects attract each other. But I don't need to imagine supernatural beings holding us to the earth. Gravity is a property of the universe. So is movement toward complexity. So is inertia. So is entropy.

These and other forces mix and mingle to create ladybugs, spider webs, asteroids, blue herons, quasars and everything else.

Meanwhile the human mind is complex enough to just scratch the surface of what's going on around us all the time. Just consider your pinky: all the tissues, cells, compounds, atoms and processes involved. It's mind-boggling.

To see more, we need to bring more to bear than clear intellect. We must approach it with all we have: mind and heart, intuitions, feeling, subtle sensing, clear thought – all of it. Not feeling to the exclusion of thought or one faculty to the exclusion of others but all of them highly functioning and integrated in a healthy way.

This is integrated or integral consciousness. It may still only scratch the surface, but it scratches deeper than rational intellect alone or intuition alone.

This integrated consciousness sees, feels, senses and observes how we are an interaction of complexity, inertia and dying. It fights these forces less and less. When flashes of creativity and inspiration arise, we flow with them. When disease and death arise, we flow with them. When we need to rest, we just rest.

In this way we stop resisting life and become more at one with life as it is.

The quality that brings this harmony is kindness. Kindness is being with things as they are rather than fighting or controlling.

This consciousness is imbued with the wonder of life. Why is there gravity? Why is there complexity? Why is there death? Why is there sustenance?

We can see these. We can measure them to a degree. But our minds and hearts have no way to answer why there is gravity, electromagnetism, butterflies, babies, mountain streams or sunsets.

Why was there a Big Bang? If the universe is 13 to 14 billion years old and we could go back 15 billion years, what would we find? What about 50 billion years ago? 500 billion? Other universes? Did they have the same natural laws?

Why is there anything? What is awareness? Who or what is asking these questions? We don't know.

But we still live and love and play within these fields of complexity, inertia and death … in things as they are.

The integrated consciousness that opens to these questions has all those qualities we described before: open, receptive, quietly joyful, curious, relaxed, inquisitive, courageous, luminous, kind, loving – all those qualities ascribed to a traditional loving God. But just as a part of all that is, not separate out there, but integrated right here.

When asked if God is real, this highly evolved objective consciousness tends to say "Yes," not because it sees supernatural powers at play but because the natural world is fascinating, joyful, awesome and luminous.

Flux and Flow

I'll leave it here. Life is still evolving. To try to resolve and bring things to closure would be out of sync with what is.

The highest consciousness is not closure, control, stillness or a metaphysical deep-freeze without light.

The highest consciousness is alive, in flux, relaxed, engaged, kind, wise, clear and luminous.

The highest reality is God or Spirit.

Or not.

Questions

After each talk I opened it up for questions and comments. The following are some of the questions asked then or at other times in response to this material.

Off the Map

The vertical gridlines point off the map and look like they fade. Is that intentional?

Yes. They also suggest convergence somewhere off the map.

As we move into the highest stages, the three perspectives converge. The highest are beyond perspective, beyond language and beyond concepts. Yet anything we say about them is bound by language. Language is inherently dualistic.

We may sense that "dissolving," "merging" and "oneness" are similar experiences. But how we name them gives them a little flavor of one of the perspectives. It's just the nature of the relative universe. The highest experience is outside the relative universe and off the map.

Integral Manipulation

If integral consciousness understands stages of consciousness other than its own and relates to people in their stages, isn't that just sophisticated manipulation?

It depends on intentions.

Consider a five-year-old child raised in a traditional Christian family. His mother dies. He asks us "Why?" Let's say our values are progressive and "not religious." How do we answer?

If we're group-centric, our progressive views feel tangible, real and true – perhaps based on science. So we answer from that perspective because it's the only one we acknowledge. We may realize he was raised with different ideas. But those barely register with us.

If we're world centric rational, we appreciate the different perspectives but still tend to project our own. We may talk about his perspectives but diminish their validity.

If we're pluralistic we appreciate the different perspectives, see the child feelings as being of the utmost importance and say what will help her feel better now.

If we're integral we implicitly take all this into account: the death, the impact it has on the child, our views, her views, how she might feel about our views, how we feel about traditional values, what's the long term picture for the child and more and respond in the moment. What we say will depend also on the nuances of the situation. It's the complexity of consideration that makes it integral more than the actual answer.

I remember seeing this in action years ago. I was part of a sangha that met in Cambridge every other Sunday afternoon. Kalu Rinpoche, a high Tibetan teacher, was with us one afternoon. He gave a talk and we asked lots of questions about Buddhism, meditation, the nature of reality and so forth.

Also with us was the four-year-old son of a couple in the sangha. He raised his hand and asked, "What about mountains, llamas and God?"

Rinpoche's answers to our questions had been refined and sophisticated. I couldn't imagine how he'd speak to these four-year-old questions.

Kalu lit up. He stretched his hand over his head, said "Himalaya" and used his finger to trace the outline of high mountains. Then he said, "llama" (the child had referred to the animal not the teacher) and moved his head forward and back in the imitation of how a llama's head moves as it walks. Then he said, "God" and raised his hands up and outward opening to the entire world as he looked up and smiled with wonder in his eyes.

The boy sat back smiling and satisfied that he was part of the adult conversation.

Kalu Rinpoche's answer was integral in that it incorporated so many different things, including being appropriate to the concrete thinking of a child. And it was as unmanipulative as I could imagine.

Integral consciousness simply acknowledges the consciousness of the other person and speaks directly to it. Whether or not it is manipulative depends on the intentions behind the words. Attempting to speak in easily understood ways is not manipulative.

Being "Saved"

How do you interpret the Christian concept of being saved?

I don't. And I wouldn't want to interpret it. Perhaps "being saved" is just an idea somebody has that they learned in Sunday School or from a local preacher. If it's just an idea in their head, then it's not very interesting.

On the other hand, maybe they had a profound experience – a deeply authentic spiritual event. Now this is interesting. Their interpretation of their experience and the language they use is "I've been saved."

So when somebody talks about being saved or meeting God or feeling God's grace I want to ask, "What was the experience like? What did you feel? What happened?"

For me personally, the concept that I can have a personal relationship with Jesus on Nazareth, this guy who walked around a few provinces in the Middle East a few millennia ago, doesn't resonate. But people can and do have quite wonderful and transformative experiences that they call "being saved." I don't want to dismiss their experience because I think I'm more intellectually sophisticated. That's just snobbery on my part.

So I don't want to interpret the concept in any general way. I want to know what a particular person has experienced when they use this kind of language. Perhaps it was a psychotic break. Perhaps it was just a passing notion. Perhaps it was a profound awakening. If they are willing to describe the experience, then we may have some interesting things to share with each other – something that is beyond language, concepts and interpretations.

Notes

As consciousness develops, it does not rise above earlier stages as much as incorporate them in a higher synthesis. I first encountered this idea in Jean Piaget's study of the development of intelligence children. Later I found it elaborated in a more detailed way in the work of Ken Wilber.

Those who are familiar with Wilber's writing will recognize his influence here. He has written many books, but the one that may have the most baring on this topic might be *Integral Spirituality* (Integral Books: Boston and London, 2007). I also found helpful an audio interview with him called *One Two Three of God*. It's available from *Sounds True*, www.soundstrue.com.

The work of Clair Graves on the development of values systems was also very helpful. You can find an overview of his work in *Spiral Dynamics* by Don Edward Beck and Christopher C. Cowan (Blackwell Publishing. 1996, 2006).

I can also see in the pages the influence of St. John of the Cross (*Dark Night of the Soul*) and Karen Armstrong (*The Case For God*). I'm also grateful to countless others who have helped me over the years including my two principle Buddhist meditation teachers, John Travis and Bante Vimalaramsi.

9151537R0

Made in the USA
Charleston, SC
15 August 2011